AUTUMN DUST

NEESHANT SRIVASTAVA

To my parents.

Contents

1. AUTUMN DUST

Come autumn and the breeze,
Brush of a little storm in swirls,
Fallen leaves green and young,
Hard and crackly a wobble,
Until shoved into an unlikely fire,
In the middle of summer and a sudden cold,
A stiff breeze and the eyes do flicker,
As dust seeps in through crevices of desire,
For a glimpse of the beautiful weather,
With the skies a shroud of white,
Autumn is the season of dreams,
When all humanity does fly,
And so do the leaves on the trees,
And the sickening weeds tall and lanky,
Or the green grass with a feather on their tails,
Let the Almighty rummage your perfection,
And throw some leaves of autumn,
To unsettle your plans and a spotless visage,
And lead you to the crackling fire,
And pickle your lawn with twigs and dust,
And leaves that once dangled high,
Broom again until a gush of wind,
Rushed to your doorstep in the dead of night,
And blows out the fire that kept you warm,

When fresh leaves fall to die,
To be one with earth,
In the long season of Autumn.

2. THE SHADOW

The shadow fell,
And I lost my path and name,
I did not remember my father,
Who had left and perhaps lost,
I lost sense of right and wrong,
I had no clue of what my mind thought,
And what my hands did,
I felt like an oppressed Indian village lass,
Too submissive and washed by sweat,
Years and years I walked alone,
Ignored and rubbed off like roasted peanut skins,
I could not see and my father left no clue,
He didn't say a word about life,
Only that my pills were somehow swallowed,
My mind cannot assimilate mind games,
They are just too low for me,
Die we will one day,
What happens around it is dust,
Eons and I survived,
To see this day,
I know now what they are talking about,
I can sense the poem,
I can feel the sadness,
And that we are all waiting for the end,

'Doing time' as they say,
And I have seen a woman,
She is just a frozen frame in time,
Locked in my upper chamber,
And I want God to ring the final bell.

3. OUT OF SORTS

Someone's out of sorts in this busy world,
Laughed at and pitied,
He has no boats to his name,
He has been taken for granted,
To slither and toss in the rampaging river,
He knows not about his plans or goals,
He is a man with a hole in his pocket,
It's easy to sway his gullible self,
He has no voice in this loud world,
He infamously goes the wrong way,
He is coaxed and lead astray easily,
He is a man with no self-respect,
For he is not a man at all,
An animal in the guise of a human,
He never said a word and when he did,
He was silenced all too easy,
And pushed like slush down a drain,
He seeks death at the earliest,
And go far away for good.

4. AND I

You were loud and clear,
And I couldn't hear You,
You were taking me somewhere,
And I was unwilling to follow,
You were trying to show me something,
And I drifted along the path,
Like impatient folks with shifting gaze,
When I was needed to hang around,
No words spoken for the end was far,
And I tossed You like a dream,
As if there was no final resting place,
My mind was a barrage of questions,
And I really doubted You,
I did not know why You had no answers,
Why You were the silent Sage,
While I was a storm of hurry,
Wanting all the answers too soon,
Your voice was loud and clear,
And I refused to listen,
Like the marrows of a foolish one,
You were trying to save me from disrepute,
And I was adamant at pointing fingers,
You asked me to wait,
For the right season,

And I could only feel the heat of summer,
Even after the rains cooled the earth,
And now I want some strength,
To wade through these tough waters,
For I know of the oasis of bliss,
And that You are waiting with open arms,
And I do love You,
For You are my saviour,
That wants me to shine,
Like the lone pole star.

5. DO YOU LOVE SOMEONE

Many years and many miles,
A voice that gave away my youth,
Me and a girl were not meant to be,
My brethren and friends around me,
Nailed it and squashed it like a watermelon,
Love was an easy whistle down the street,
That a fool could never miss,
Many fell around me,
Each one with a dame so sweet,
Like catching butterflies after a warm rain,
They just wished into outstretched palms,
Fluttering like they could fly away,
My youth passed by like dumb charades,
Not pushing too hard to force a point,
My body hanging loose like a topless belly,
To throw away eyes that crashed by accident,
On a pathos of remorse and regret,
I did not fit into the flesh market,
Much like a teacher I knew,
That was much bulkier than me,
Now the years have flown,
And I am too old for the new,

An 'uncle' for youngsters,
A father without a son,
A grandfather without a grandson,
Looking at dames is a crime,
Sleeping with them would be,
Sleeping with my own daughter,
I do bid adieu to life now,
Fare thee well young ducklings,
Life can be fun and easy if you want,
And it will be, I know,
Your waters do not run deep, I can tell,
You'll get over the hang over someday too soon,
Like all humanity does,
But that cushion at your back,
Shall keep you warm,
You have toiled hard after all,
In the days of the flesh.

6. THAT SQUEAKY LITTLE BIRD

That squeaky little bird by my window sill,
Eyes of pearls and tender wings,
You know not of a far-off place,
You'd rather hop on soft branches,
With your family of squeaky littles ones,
You twitter in my ear each morning,
And at dusk when I rest uneasy,
To hear you say something and leave,
Before those hands of grasping shadows,
Spread their web so dangerously close,
I wish I were a bird like you,
That wished for no more than a grain or two,
And sat all day on a breezy tree,
Eyes half shut to disappear in the darkness,
You will not listen to me,
You will not come near me,
Haven't you mistaken what's in my heart,
And overlooked the love I have for you,
I cannot not explain the monster in me,
I just want to see you fly away now,
To your own secret nook,
Far away from prying eyes,

That have only learnt destruction and damage,
Heartless with a heart,
Please sing me a song,
And come as close as you can,
You, squeaky little angel by my window sill,
By morning and dusk,
I have found a fleeting friend.

7. A LOVELY GARDEN

God blessed me with a lovely garden,
It has trees with leaves that shine,
After a bout of rain or a receding autumn,
A green lawn with soft grass,
That lends a cushion to tired feet,
Flower beds with flowers that come and go,
Stumps of trees that cast a dark shadow once,
On the electricity wires that hung low,
Or the huge transformers with their fall,
When they stood tall for a mighty lunge,
The brown soil that wets and dries to the whims,
Of an uncertain rain,
The garden of mine fills me with life,
When I fail in a land of freakish heights,
Where people occupy themselves with low,
And brackish games that seem too gutless,
And without a voice,
As they have to hide in a nameless corner,
For the crimes they have committed,
I love the green and blue skies above it,
It makes me gay when I am sad,
For no fault of mine,
And tells me of stories when I shall rise,
To the place I deserve in life,

Welcome to my garden of little birds,
That hop on the lawn and pick on a puddle,
They remind me of how glorious life is,
And that I shall fly away one day,
To a land that they probably know.

8. THAT STRETCH OF ROAD

I shall never forget that stretch of road,
That was my only companion of many years,
I walked up and down each evening,
When the sun was soft and the moon did hide,
Among the lush trees swept by the breeze,
The trees grew thin each passing season,
As they camouflaged the stretch of road,
And the walker entered a different world,
With the taste of the unknown and surreal,
I stole my way in lonely footsteps,
To be with the broken road,
That carried no wheels or any noise,
Lost and abandoned it lay aloof,
To be unnoticed and unsung,
Much like the story of my life,
Yet it brought me delight with a rush of wind,
To make the sagging branches dangle low,
Until it was lush again at the opportune season,
To be replete with flowers and new leaves,
My tears ran dry each time,
I happened to pass by that stretch,
And filled me with joy,

When I was in deep sorrow,
And could not pull myself out of my grief,
To sing again in the moment,
And forget how my life was slipping away,
I walked that stretch for more than ten years,
All alone wishing for someone,
Like I had been outcast and refused,
To be in the family of friends,
And to gather the simple joys that all possess,
This stretch of road was carving something,
Out of me that I couldn't see,
Perhaps the Almighty wished it this way,
That beautiful stretch of road,
I shall never forget,
Was my home in paradise.

9. AND SHE DIED

I could not get over her loss,
She was my mother,
My life had ended with her,
I felt death everywhere for years,
Like I too had died with her,
My brother saw death at every corner,
Life cannot get over a huge loss so soon,
Even though the wheels are still in spin,
Like nothing ever happened,
The same milkman with cold milk,
The same hawker of a busy world,
The same faces in a new day,
The sun, moon and stars,
Making me feel that nothing had changed,
Something in me was lost,
And I just tried to overlook the damage,
It will take me years to get back,
The cheer in my eyes,
And to live the rest of my life.

10. SHE CAME TO ME

I have lived the life of a bird,
Too often on my wings,
Lost somewhere in the distant skies,
Until I discovered ages hence,
What I had been missing all along,
And I want it dearly now,
The warmth of a touch,
Off those slender fingers,
I am reminded of a love that never was,
I was a young lad then, too young,
And she came to me after my fiftieth,
And I have never been in love before,
And I denied and still deny,
For she was a princess meant for kings,
And I a street side beggar with an empty bowl,
She was young as young can be,
The most beautiful woman I ever saw,
And she might have been married that year,
To a wealthy man by money and soul,
And she might have had beautiful children,
After a year or two,
And I forgot her for she was my teacher,
At school when I began my studies,
She punished me with all her wrath,

She was too cruel to me,
But I took solace in her beauty,
And her sweet perfume,
When she twisted my ears,
With polished finger nails,
Why has she appeared after forty-three years,
Is this some divine prank,
That the Almighty is playing with me,
Don't show me dreams that can never come true,
I'd rather carry my mantle of chapped fingers,
And dress in tatters,
Than to hold the hands of a princess,
Of the heavenly skies,
I have paid the price for being a recluse,
And now I must live through what remains,
Of a most worthless life,
With a constant cloud of sadness in its skies,
That never let the blue from its coat,
Live long my beautiful lady,
May God bless you.

11. OCEAN OF BLUE

The sky is an ocean of blue again,
Many days of lifeless and bland,
Clouds of death with buckets now and again,
As the slush rose with an unbearable stench,
That no human can possibly bear,
I was locked in my room for days,
As the water in my front yard began to rot,
It could not find its way out or dry,
What an unforgiving country this,
Like a forsaken and remote village,
When the refuse is too high,
Yet there is some hope today,
The waters have dried,
The blue sky will burn to pale by noon,
As the sun beats hard on the ground,
And the wind is not too bad,
The trees wiggle to bursts of the wind,
In fresh green leaves that make me forget,
The horrors of this place,
And an evening walk is all I wish for,
When the wind sings sweet,
And caresses my face and body,
Like a soft and tender touch,
To a promise of better days to come,

Never mind the slump here and there,
It's all in the game,
And the Mother is all too kind,
To rid Her children off the discomfort,
And bless them for the remaining life,
To stick around in Her lap,
And not think of leaving Her,
The ocean of blue never looked so pretty.

12. THE DARK FOREST

The forest is too dark,
They cannot see,
They raise their hands and bend their knees,
Never did they hear a voice,
The voice of ages that cannot be heard,
For they have never known,
A life beyond their sunken life,
Too far in logic they act like they know,
The divine and the Holy are mere lies,
A straight line is all they can afford,
Too fearful of themselves,
Of a voice that spoke and was silenced,
Food and clothing are their crown of pride,
They have hungry ones to feed,
Atheists have never known,
As they grope for proof in vain,
For God does not appear at the local market,
No money or wealth can bring Him,
Have you seen God?
Is the general query,
The forest is too dark my friend,
There is no room for light anymore,
You are completely lost forever,
For is takes effort to dispel the darkness,

And see some light flickering somewhere,
For without light, you are nothing but dead,
As you walk flashing your possessions to the world,
For you there was no God ever,
And there will be none,
Be prepared for your afterlife.

13. IN MY ROOM

I watched the world go by,
In my airy room,
My window is shut and frosted,
I hear the circle of breeze on my face,
I haven't moved for years,
Ever since my mother was gone,
They say how can you sit so still,
Hearing the wheels and the honks,
I have no queen on my bed,
I am sitting like trudging through life,
It is a passage enroute so dry,
There are no cheers no song,
Falling on my parched ears,
I am known to be the violent one,
And I have cursed my untimely outbursts,
For I have hurt a lot of people,
And they say it's hard to change,
When love can make the rigid,
Bend their backs,
And teach them the softest of melodies,
That shook new born flowers of spring,
In a heavenly soft breeze,
If I am love in my veins,
Then where does this madness come from,

I was a spit of fire when required,
But now the embers are cold,
There is no need to scare the death of others,
I'd rather perish than to hurt others,
May God help me to be kind,
I have sinned for too long,
Let no one be a victim of my wrath,
And I do have love for all,
My slip down recklessness I regret,
For I was too casual,
Forgive me for my sins,
My room is my redemption,
I can never leave its shadow.

14. LONG AGO

Long ago I waited for her,
Like a fool I refused to see,
On a promise that became trite with time,
I was pushing away life in my youth,
Too obstinate for unknown reasons,
As I waited for her,
With no sign until grey,
Fit to be a father to my children,
God was silent like He always is,
I stayed away from the jaunty crowd,
In a quiet corner of the world,
Too conscious of the great ridicule,
That might have hit me in a crowded city,
Where the world finds solace and fun,
And the great carnival called life,
This is my destiny I have come to realize,
Some people have it and some don't,
These silent walls and the air of doom,
Will show no mercy for a broken heart,
If only I could fill my days,
With the thought of my loved one,
For every man does have a woman, I hear,
I stay calm and wait for the finish,
When I shall flee and perhaps,

Open my eyes in the laps of God,
For I have carried sorrow too intense,
That was too heard to bear,
And if the world has left me alone,
To die an unknown death,
So be it,
How much love does a man carry,
In his forsaken heart,
That has never been loved before,
And who died for a drop of love,
From some longing eyes,
I hang on the cross burning and in pain,
I have failed to hear from the Lord,
Bring me those eyes before I close my eyes,
My body cannot hold on longer,
I am breathing hard,
If You can hear,
May Your Kingdom on earth flourish,
And bring better times,
For unknown struggles,
We need You,
Amen.

15. THAT IS YOUR FAULT

You are too sweet and good,

Your heart weeps for teary eyes,

What did you make for yourself in this world,

And they hate you with all their might,

You gave so sweetly that the divine wept,

Of your life and a simple truth,

That is often unheard and forgotten,

These people have lives if you should know,

Tangled and mess they crash and burn,

As you rose higher by your simple act,

And spoke of a simple truth,

That no one ever could spare an inch,

For anyone at all,

For love is a difficult thing,

And the fire too thick for souls,

To melt away and become pure,

And love is a blasphemous world,

It's roaming around on the streets,

It's the pick-up girl too keen to lend her flesh,

For the definitive moan in ample darkness,

To transport her to earthly heaven,

And tear her insides like her dreams,

As she drips wet with exhilaration,
Love has never been so low,
And spoken of this way by every new blood,
You softly destroyed yourself,
Crushed and tortured like evil,
Yet please remember,
God loves you,
And many others love you,
Don't mind a few,
To be good is not your fault.

16. THAT SACRED NIGHT

I have seen the Holy come,
In a world that was high and aloof,
I hardly saw the faces and hearts in flight,
Until the grand night,
And my folks sat around me,
And the woman that I dreamt of,
Too eager for vows and wedlock,
I stood stunned to a woman I had forgotten,
Long ago as a boy in shorts,
I did feel something I was sure,
And it all came back like a blessing,
After a rough period of ringing death,
When my grief would not set me free,
And pain was second nature,
Like a sinner sinless,
Many years of deep peril,
Until they declared me permanently dead,
Not before that grand night,
When I was one with a woman from heaven,
And a lavish dinner was laid on the table,
And smiles echoed and circled the room,
My parents were a witness to the night,

She stayed with me for months,
Before heading towards a broken star,
As I descended to the ground,
To find a broken boat and dusty path,
In an ocean of silence and gloom,
To start again to build a tent of hope,
To carve out a home after the vicious storm,
All alone with my folks rested,
All I need is some time before I am up,
To never forget the glimpses of glimpse,
After the take off into the heavenly skies,
I am here to make some amends,
And cast a shadow before I go,
And I know what's coming,
To be so sure of my steps,
Has taken me a lifetime of burn,
Until I found a reason for existence,
However insignificant that may be,
And whatever the good Lord chose to do,
Is a privilege much the same,
To be flighty and high,
And witness the sacred night,
Was worth the mess I found myself in,
And as for the givers of pain,
And the pleasure seekers that know laughter,
And inflict torture on others,
While the other smothers in incessant pain,
You have never seen and will never see,
The glory of God,

And a life is too short for the devil,
They are too involved and trapped,
In their own web like hanging spiders,
They cannot move lest the web snaps,
I may have none today,
But I have seen those soft skies,
That change hue to a different era,
And bring out the hidden beauty,
That resides in the soul,
Much like the sacred night,
And the woman of curly locks,
And beautiful skin,
Too happy to hold my hands forever.

17. WALK AWAY

I did not know when I turned young,
Like sneaky seasons that swept too soon,
I too longed for someone,
When the search began,
Too far away in a boy's only school,
I longed for a glimpse of feminine eyes,
Many restless hearts knew the girl's school,
A few blocks away they were there,
After school hours with hungry eyes,
While I knew my way home,
I have walked away ever since,
For reasons that are hard to explain,
Even to the selfish part of me,
I'd rather leave someone alone,
Even if someone felt the heat of my heart,
I thus have many unfinished love stories,
To my diseased name,
They say if someone truly loves you,
Then they do return no matter what,
And I am the greatest fool in a world,
That is all too sure of everything,
Like love is a dime in their pockets,
That is all too revealing and palpable,
As they switch faces like the morning paper,

Nobody knows or even wants to know,
That love is not the games we play in bed,
Or some slave to our beck and call,
For one, true love never comes,
For it does not exist,
And we live unhappy lives,
To pour our frustration on others,
And make our lives toxic,
And the chemicals rip our insides,
Have you ever done anything for anyone?
Asked the sailor of high seas,
Out of love or affection,
Death is not an option on high seas,
And life does not even exist,
Only a long stretch of pain,
As we burn in the holy fire,
Love is what no human can,
Not because they are less,
But for they never will,
We survive on peanuts,
And on peanuts we shall forever,
For that man that walked far,
Was given a greater fire to burn,
And a longer fire to burn,
And God made sure He did not spare him,
Don't talk of love,
It shall decorate the books like it has,
Over the centuries,
Get ready for your sweetheart,

She's got you in a groove,
And there are plenty more,
To last a lifetime.

18. PERISHING HEAD

I met an old man when I was a boy,
He said he saw the perishing head,
Of the Mahatma,
When the great man was addressing a crowd,
Seldom have known or seen,
A man that gifted his life to his nation,
He was not artist, mathematician, poet,
Wore silk, satin or turned an Englishman,
He had no land, money or belongings,
He walked the land he called his own motherland,
He fought for the soil that gave him life,
Yet they tarnished and threw scum,
In his own land by his own people,
They blamed him for the plight of the nation,
They called him the dirtiest man that could be,
That worked for his image and caused civil unrest,
For there was a time,
When Bapu raised his hand for a cause,
For he was disenchanted over something,
And the entire nation from the south,
The east, west and the north,
Rushed on the streets with a fire in their belly,
To listen to Bapu,
And set things right at the earliest,

Such was the truth of the man,
In a bag of bones,
For every voice that has ever been raised,
For the sake of humanity,
Has been silenced in all brutality,
Just like Gandhi was,
As horrific tales still do their rounds,
And the children already hate Bapu,
All the rumours about his personal life,
Let us kindle the truth in our souls,
If we ever have the courage to do so,
A world without a spine,
Is a world that is lost forever,
Why pretend to be human,
When you can never be one,
Gandhi comes once in centuries,
As flesh and blood as anyone ever born,
Yet greater than and holy as the divine,
Even God shudders to see such courage,
Don't talk of life,
You'll never know what it is,
Before it leaves you all grey and old,
But Gandhi lives on,
And is a man for the ages.

19. THEY WANT TO BE

They want to be counted among the greats,
They want to leave a mark on the way,
They want to discard the common robe,
They want to be the chosen one,
They are ready to bare and dare,
Why then only a few among a few,
Ever tread on that slender road,
With the heat to melt the human flesh,
And the thorns prickly and tipped with venom,
Enough to force an early exit,
And wallow on scrumptious streets,
With mellow trees dressed in colour,
And the blue waters that thrash the cold sand,
And touch the feet like a scented balm,
Do not play around with life, if you will,
Your madness is your own choice,
While others navigate your insanity,
With handcuffs and meticulous asylums,
And your mental asymmetry is a game for some,
While you make no sense of living,
Do not try to follow the divine,
He'll crush You to death,
And a silent cremation if that ever happens,
When He wished that you survive,

To see the end of the great abnormality,
Thrust on you quite intentionally,
To see if you carry the strength to survive,
And fight till the very end,
Don't be surprised then if you saw no divine,
And your life turned out to be pure slavery,
And you still carry a dying wish,
To be among the greats,
Life is too short to lament,
Prepare for death if you are through,
You'll be a part of this crazy world again,
But it maybe a while until that happens,
For souls aren't born as humans too soon,
For now, it's time to assess,
For God is the greatest truth,
And we cannot hide on the final day,
As we succumb to our deeds,
And wish for grace.

20. TRUE TO WORD

Many days and many miles,
I never knew that the hands above me,
Would desert me to ashes and dust,
While I educate myself, my only student,
And think of things that walk with me,
For a while before blown into the wind,
What are these people talking about,
Why do these people look so worried,
Someone is trying hard to make us immortal,
Love is for sale and the young ones know plenty,
Breakups, prenups, threesome, twosome and some cream,
A journey that has not even begun,
Has seen hands tied together and promises,
Only to be broken the week after,
Success is money and its byproducts,
With illicit loopholes that will not question,
The easy and quick way to own a villa,
Before you see off your teens in your mind,
We have forgotten Christ,
Or will very soon,
Word has value,
For love is the word of truth,
And if couples end us enslaving the other,
For the fear of break up,

Then it is the lack of love,
That does not come like it is on its way,
In most cases it never even comes,
And the money cannot buy some love,
Like some fish in the fish market,
While we attempt at being immortal,
Funny how out little brains,
Makes grandiose plans in a short span,
But a habit is hard to give up,
Especially when it's too late,
Let's instead save enough for posterity,
Love is probably meant for some other age.